HIDING BEHIND
Lipstick

HIDING BEHIND *Lipstick*

A Woman's Guide to Unveiling Her Truth

Chauntele M. Holley

ISBN-13 (paperback): 978-1-329-92240-2

Printed in the United States of America

Editor: Ink Pen Diva Manuscript Critique Services, LLC

Book Cover & Interior Design: Purposely Created Publishing

Dedication

This book is dedicated to my grandmother, Juanita Bullard Faulk.

Even in an Alzheimer's state you knew that "I belonged to you." Your nurturing spirit was one of a kind. I miss you.

xoxo

Table of Contents • • • • • • • • • • • • •

Dedication v

Acknowledgements ix

Introduction 1

Pledge 4

31 Days of Positive Affirmations for Your Life . . . 6

Meet the Author 68

About Lipstick Chatter™ 71

Acknowledgements · · · · · · · · · · ·

Father God you have shown me favor once again. Thank you for the courage and vision to write this guide for women. I will never take this platform for granted. I will use it as a ministry to uplift and inspire women all over the world.

A huge THANK YOU to my #1 supporter's:

My mother, Diane White and my daughter, Jazmine Montgomery.

Mom, I want to thank you for every sacrifice made and the unconditional love shown to your only child. I am everything that I am because of you.

Jazmine, I love you more than the air I breathe. Looking at you is like seeing my reflection in the mirror although the image is bigger and brighter. I am proud of you and I'm so grateful that God chose me to be your Mom.

I love you both with everything that I AM.

To my confidant, Shawn Davis, through the highs and the lows I can always count on you. Thank you from the bottom of my heart. Know that, everything that you seek is actually seeking you. My love is endless.

To my dad, I'd give anything to hear you laugh one more time! I miss you!

To my aunts, Jennifer Faulk, Whilamena Faulk and Doris Faulk, I've learned so much from each of you. Thank you for your individual roles in my life. Your love and support means the world to me. I love you all with my whole heart.

To my cousin LaDawn Faulk who is more like a sister to me, I love you to the moon and back. Thank you for always being there for me. Your support keeps me striving for greatness.

To my cousins Natalie Sanders, Aletra Harvey, and Lea Banks, thank you all from the bottom of my heart for always being there and being the prayer warriors that you are. You all keep me covered.

To my cousin/son Terrence Faulk, you have made me so very proud. I love you Navy Man.

To my best friends for life, Karen Robinson and Germaine Walker, I don't know what I would do without either of you! I attribute the way I've grown in relationships to each of you; thank you for always

being there for me, challenging me to be my best and loving me in spite of me.

Special shout out to my Dope Chicks™, each of you are like family. You are some of the strongest women I know. God has blessed me with your sisterhood. I love you.

To my spiritual sister, Pauline Hightower our connection is indescribable. Thank you for always being there to help me pick up the pieces.

To my friends, Tracey Williams, Fatima Arthur, Naysheia Richbourgh, Dwane Heyward, Michelle Flowers, Carlotta Crayton and Kimberly Staton – thanks for being Lipstick Chatter advocates. You all go hard for my brand and I love you for it.

To my Mahogany Book Club members, it seems like it's been a lifetime. What a true testament of sisterhood, thank you guys for hanging in there.

To my Lipstick Chatter community, thanks for rocking with me. I feel the love and I'm sending it right back to you.

To my clients and mentees, thank you for trusting me.

To my business bestie, Kemberli Stephenson, you are Heaven sent. Thank you for pouring into me and my business wholeheartedly.

To each and every one of my friends and family members, my love for you runs deep. I'm forever grateful to have each of you in my life. Thank you for your support, guidance, influence and love. I'm forever humbled.

To my editor, Tamika L. Sims, with Ink Pen Diva Manuscript Critique Services, LLC, I appreciate you.

To everyone who has purchased my book – may your life be forever changed!

And last but certainly not least, to everyone that has come in my life and left, I sincerely thank you for every lesson and for teaching me the gift of goodbye. I am a better woman because of you and my only hope is that I left you better than I found you. God bless you all.

"You were born to have everything you desire. You just have to go get it!"

~ **Chauntele M. Holley**

Introduction

To every woman who thinks it is over for her. Within these pages, you will find positive affirmations and quotes designed to uncover your truth and heal your spirit. The affirmations provided will serve as your guide. I invite you to tap into the power of your voice and speak over every area of your life, children, finances, health and wellness.

What I have discovered on my life's journey is sometimes our world is framed by what others have said to us. Sometimes we allow these things whether positive or negative, to impact us and chart our course. Today, I say to you, the buck stops here. It is time to get off of the proverbial train and back on the right track. The track you determine. The track God has predestined.

Hiding Behind Lipstick was created with you in my mind and heart. Lipstick, as with any type of makeup, is designed to mask and cover. It is designed to dress-up the outward appearance.

Makeup does nothing for our inner woman; it does not do anything to dress up our hearts. It's time to remove the masks and rid yourself of the layers. It's time to wipe away the red, nude or pink that adorns your lips.

No longer are we dressing up the wounds. Let's put down the salve and remove the Band-Aid. It's time to look at the root cause of the pain and source of your hurt.

The first step is to make an agreement with yourself by signing the pledge provided on the next page. Signing this pledge and making the agreement, does not mean that you will get it right the first or second time. It means that every time you fall short, you make the decision to recommit yourself. You must vow to never live another year broken. You must vow to be whole and be made over again. You must commit to affirming who you are every second, minute and instant, you feel unworthy or insecure.

Within these pages are the keys to unlocking your best yet!

Come along and take this journey with me, tissue in hand, and let's begin to wipe away all traces of any attempt to cover up.

Take a deep breath and turn the page.

Pledge

From this day forward, I, _____
commit to uncovering my truth and beginning the healing process of loving myself just as I am. I will create healthy morning rituals.

I will stop apologizing and reliving my past. I will take off the barriers I've placed on myself as well as the limiting beliefs. I will be obedient to my calling and not make any excuses about where God is taking me. I will not take no for an answer.

I will set goals for my life. I will believe in myself more. I will learn to uplift my sisters. I will rebuke the spirit of envy and jealousy. I will be more transparent about who I am and not fear being judged. I will stand unapologetic in my truth. Who I am today is only a glimpse of who I am becoming. If I fall short, I will recommit to this process. I am ready to do the work.

Sincerely,

_____

A New Journey

31 DAYS OF POSITIVE AFFIRMATIONS FOR YOUR LIFE

• • •

On a scale of 1-10, how strong is your faith? ____

REMEMBER THIS...

When God has ordained you to do something, you must act on it! It's not your job to figure out HOW it's going to work. He's already worked it out.

REPEAT AFTER ME...

I **believe** everything that I seek is seeking me.

Unveil your truth...

Day 1

I choose to live my life in peace.

• • •

In silence you will hear the truth and begin to find solutions.

DAY 1

Take 10 minutes today to sit in silence
and seek the truth. The truth is…

_____

_____

_____

_____

_____

_____

_____

_____

_____

_____

_____

Day 2

I AM going after everything that belongs to me.

• • •

Fear arises when you are about to do something really dope. You must do it afraid.

DAY 2

List 3 of your major fears.

_____

_____

_____

_____

_____

_____

_____

_____

_____

_____

_____

Day 3

I choose to release the weight of shame, hurt,
defeat, fear, hate and self-doubt.

• • •

**The most beautiful thing about knowing who you
are is never having to prove it.**

DAY 4

What have you been trying to prove and why?

_____

_____

_____

_____

_____

_____

_____

_____

_____

_____

_____

Day 4

I AM who God says I am.

• • •

You will never be a victim and a queen.

DAY 4

Write 5 powerful words you will begin to use to describe yourself. I AM...

_____

_____

_____

_____

_____

_____

_____

_____

_____

Day 5

I will trust myself more.

• • •

**When you get caught up in your feelings,
you have to take a step back and remember
who in the hell you really are.**

DAY 5

Take a look in the mirror and describe the image that you see staring back at you.

_____

_____

_____

_____

_____

_____

_____

_____

_____

_____

Day 6

I will not waste time proving my worth to others.

. . .

Stop wasting time on idle conversations and relationships that serve no purpose in your life.

List 3 people, places and/or things currently
in your life that take up time but provide
no value in your life:

_____

_____

_____

_____

_____

_____

_____

_____

_____

_____

Day 7

Where I've been will not stop me from
where I'm going.

• • •

**Covering up who you are stops you from getting
what you need.**

Today I forgive myself for:

_____

_____

_____

_____

_____

_____

_____

_____

_____

_____

_____

Day 8

I will pick up the pieces and make the best out of my life with what I have.

• • •

There is a process to healing and the first step is acknowledgment.

DAY 8

I am totally grateful for my gift of:

_____

_____

_____

_____

_____

_____

_____

_____

_____

_____

_____

Day 9

I will do what I didn't have the courage
to do yesterday.

• • •

**Never dismiss your dream for fear that you've
missed your window of opportunity.**

List 3 people you need to connect with and why:

_____

_____

_____

_____

_____

_____

_____

_____

_____

_____

_____

Day 10

I will do what God has called me to do.

• • •

**You can't be everything to everybody
and nothing to yourself.**

Write 40 things that bring you joy:

_____

_____

_____

_____

_____

_____

_____

_____

_____

_____

_____

_____

Day 11

I AM worthy of all that I desire.

• • •

Forgive yourself for staying too long.
Forgive yourself for not speaking up.
Forgive yourself for not loving you more.

God has already forgiven me and now it's time
I forgive myself for:

_____

_____

_____

_____

_____

_____

_____

_____

_____

_____

Day 12

I AM loved and supported.

• • •

**The devil isn't always busy;
it could be the company you keep.**

DAY 12

Write down the people in your immediate circle
and what purpose they serve in your life:

_____

_____

_____

_____

_____

_____

_____

_____

_____

_____

Day 13

I AM unstoppable.

• • •

**God hasn't only given you the vision,
He has made provision.**

What will you do differently today to seek
a different outcome?

_____

_____

_____

_____

_____

_____

_____

_____

_____

_____

Day 14

I lack nothing.

• • •

When your mindset shifts from victim to survivor you will experience God's grace and unmerited favor every day.

DAY 14

Give thanks for every gift you encounter today.

_____

_____

_____

_____

_____

_____

_____

_____

_____

_____

_____

Day 15

My peace is non-negotiable.

• • •

Stop trying to prove yourself to people and surrender to God's call over your life.

Create a list of 15 things that bring you peace:

_____

_____

_____

_____

_____

_____

_____

_____

_____

_____

_____

Day 16

I AM willing and ready to make the necessary changes today.

• • •

We never become who we want by remaining who we are.

DAY 16

What can you implement in your life today
that will bring about change?

_____

_____

_____

_____

_____

_____

_____

_____

_____

_____

Day 17

I will no longer wait for people to give me
permission to live my life.

• • •

**Searching for happiness outside of yourself is like
looking for yourself in a crowded room.**

DAY 17

What are you willing to change in the area
of your life that you've been settling in?

_____

_____

_____

_____

_____

_____

_____

_____

_____

_____

Day 18

I will surround myself with successful people.

• • •

Your goals are still relevant.

DAY 18

How could a coach or mentor help you
stay focused on your goals?

_____

_____

_____

_____

_____

_____

_____

_____

_____

_____

Day 19

Nothing that I have done will stop me
from my destiny.

• • •

**When we become aware of who we are and
whose we are, things begin to fall into perspective.**

Create your personal mission statement.
What do you want to be known for?

_____

_____

_____

_____

_____

_____

_____

_____

_____

_____

Day 20

I AM the competition.

• • •

Once you start loving everything about yourself,
you'll stop comparing yourself to other women
and you become the competition.

If you were at your best, what would you
be doing right now?

Day 21

I AM no longer available for people
with manipulative spirits.

• • •

**The person you've given power to will always
have control over you.**

DAY 21

What are you most insecure about?

_____

_____

_____

_____

_____

_____

_____

_____

_____

_____

_____

Day 22

I vow to love myself more today than yesterday.

• • •

**Free yourself from the crazy idea that you
have to be like, look like or speak like
someone else to fit in.**

DAY 22

Spend extra time today with your hair
and your appearance. What makes you unique?

_____

_____

_____

_____

_____

_____

_____

_____

_____

_____

Day 23

I AM the priority.

• • •

You bring about what you think about.
You speak about what consumes your mind!

Start thinking and speaking of the good things
you want to see manifest in your life and start
expecting them.

DAY 23

Write an affirmation for each day
of the week and repeat it to yourself
when negative thoughts creep in.

_____

_____

_____

_____

_____

_____

_____

_____

_____

Day 24

I have my own special gifts to share
with the world.

• • •

**Now is not the time to compare your chapter 2
to someone else's chapter 20.**

Write down 3 things you have overcome:

_____

_____

_____

_____

_____

_____

_____

_____

_____

_____

_____

Day 25

I AM focused on building better relationships.

• • •

**Set yourself free by forgiving someone,
even if that someone is you.**

What healthy attributes will you contribute
to your relationships?

_____

_____

_____

_____

_____

_____

_____

_____

_____

_____

Day 26

I AM no longer making excuses for the things that
I cannot change.

• • •

**Free yourself from the boundaries you've
placed on yourself.**

What has been your greatest life lesson
and what did it teach you?

_____

_____

_____

_____

_____

_____

_____

_____

_____

_____

Day 27

Today I make the decision to become my best self.

• • •

**Settling holds you hostage to everything
you don't believe in.**

Reflect on the things you know for sure
about yourself.

_____

_____

_____

_____

_____

_____

_____

_____

_____

_____

Day 28

Today I will face my fear head on.

• • •

**Most are not afraid of failing.
It's actually success that scares the hell
out of them.**

Find an accountability partner that will hold you
accountable to your goals.

_____

_____

_____

_____

_____

_____

_____

_____

_____

_____

Day 29

Today I will do what I wasn't prepared
to do yesterday.

• • •

God has anointed you for this assignment.

List 3 immediate action steps you can take
to get closer to your goals:

_____

_____

_____

_____

_____

_____

_____

_____

_____

_____

Day 30

I will never have to chase what's meant for me.

• • •

Once you slow down to see just how beautiful you are on the inside, greatness will show up on the outside.

DAY 30

Read Psalm 46:10 and journal your thoughts.

_____

_____

_____

_____

_____

_____

_____

_____

_____

_____

_____

_____

Day 31

My destiny is not tied to anyone or anything behind me.

• • •

Put down the broken pieces from yesterday.

DAY 31

Today I choose to release:

_____

_____

_____

_____

_____

_____

_____

_____

_____

_____

Trust Your Journey...

REMEMBER THIS...
Focusing on the past blocks every great
opportunity for the future.

REPEAT AFTER ME...
I **will** trust my journey.

Meet the Author • • • • • • • • • • •

CHAUNTELE M. HOLLEY
is the founder and visionary of lifestyle brand, Lipstick Chatter, a holistic movement for purpose-driven women seeking CHANGE, CLARITY and the CONFIDENCE™ to live an unapologetic lifestyle.

With more than 20 years of corporate experience as an Executive Support Professional, Ms. Holley has helped support the business leaders of major Fortune 100 companies & now brings that same level of purpose and passion to her peers via the Lipstick Chatter brand. She nurtures her tribe through several coaching platforms; accountability workshops, signature annual women's retreat (A Woman's Worth) and one-on-one coaching.

Not only is Chauntele a thought leader, motivator, and smart business woman but she is also the mastermind behind the newly launched online sisterhood academy 'Dope Chicks Unite'™! A membership academy for D.O.P.E. (Designed to Operate in Purpose Every day) women of all ethnicities to come together and build stronger communities and relationships in love and prosperity!

A natural born leader, Chauntele's mission is to motivate and inspire women to believe they can achieve more in their lives. She teaches women how to move from merely existing to conquering their fears and walking boldly in their purpose! Her coaching programs go beyond the basics and dig deep into her client's challenges and obstacles to assure they achieve results. She's is also author of *A Journey Within: 6 Keys to a Renewed Life!*

Ms. Holley was born and raised in Hempstead, NY and currently resides in the Raleigh, NC area.

WHAT IS LIPSTICK CHATTER?

Lipstick Chatter is a holistic movement for purpose-driven women seeking change, clarity and the confidence to live an unapologetic lifestyle. Lipstick Chatter  was founded in January 2014 when I'd hit a tough spot in my life and felt like giving up. I wasn't suicidal. I was numb! Numb to all of the things going on around me. I knew I couldn't stay in that state of mind. But there had been so much going on it took me a while to see my way through.

I was focused on what happened (past) versus all of the possibilities (present and future) that I should have been focused on. The loss of my job, the heartbreak and betrayal of trust had all become too much.

I began to seek God and ask Him what my purpose was. I was led to blogging. I would create and share inspiration for women daily. As I began to blog and respond to my tribe I was led into mentoring and coaching women who were just like me. This was something I had done all of my life without a title. I've always been an advocate for sisterhood. I push women to dream big, achieve their goals and to also live their lives to the fullest.

I love to see women win, especially those who come out of circumstances where it didn't look like they had a shot.

Lipstick Chatter hosts an annual women's retreat – A Woman's Worth™! This retreat is centered on the renewing of the heart, mind, body and spirit. It is a time for women to come together for a weekend of relaxation, networking, sisterhood, and bonding. This is where Dope Chicks Unite was born.

If that's you and you'd like to join the movement follow me on social media. I'd love to connect with you.

CONNECT WITH ME
@LipstickChatter

BOOK ME TO SPEAK AT YOUR NEXT EVENT!

Send an email to:
lipstickchatter@gmail.com

LEARN MORE ABOUT CHAUNTELE AT:

www.LipstickChatter.com

CPSIA information can be obtained at www.ICGtesting.com
Printed in the USA
BVOW02s2116210416

445150BV00001B/1/P